T0149700

FROM CHAIN-SMOKER TO NON-SMOKER

Easy Steps to Quit Smoking for Good and Never Look Back

SUBASH THAPA

BALBOA.PRESS

A DIVISION OF HAY HOUSE

Copyright © 2019 Subash Thapa.

All rights reserved. No part of this book may be used or reproduced by any means,
graphic, electronic, or mechanical, including photocopying, recording, taping or by
any information storage retrieval system without the written permission of the author
except in the case of brief quotations embodied in critical articles and reviews.

Balboa Press books may be ordered through booksellers or by contacting:

Balboa Press
A Division of Hay House
1663 Liberty Drive
Bloomington, IN 47403
www.balboapress.com.au
1 (877) 407-4847

Because of the dynamic nature of the Internet, any web addresses or links contained in
this book may have changed since publication and may no longer be valid. The views
expressed in this work are solely those of the author and do not necessarily reflect the
views of the publisher, and the publisher hereby disclaims any responsibility for them.

The author of this book does not dispense medical advice or prescribe the use of any
technique as a form of treatment for physical, emotional, or medical problems without the
advice of a physician, either directly or indirectly. The intent of the author is only to offer
information of a general nature to help you in your quest for emotional and spiritual well-
being. In the event you use any of the information in this book for yourself, which is your
constitutional right, the author and the publisher assume no responsibility for your actions.

Any people depicted in stock imagery provided by Getty Images are models,
and such images are being used for illustrative purposes only.
Certain stock imagery © Getty Images.

Cover Image Credit: Boonyachoat and Thithawat_s

Print information available on the last page.

ISBN: 978-1-5043-1995-9 (sc)
ISBN: 978-1-5043-2125-9 (hc)
ISBN: 978-1-5043-1994-2 (e)

Balboa Press rev. date: 03/28/2020

For my mum and dad; my wife, Batoul; and my children, Noah and Ilias. You are all an inspiration for me, and I love you dearly.

*From Chain-Smoker to Non-Smoke*r's Mission

One life saved equals one generation saved. One person saved from smoking equals thirty to forty other people who have a chance to save theirs.

In addition to donating a percentage of royalties to charities, copies of books will be donated to individuals who need them.

If we can save one person from smoking, we can protect generations that may follow. Children growing up will observe adults in their life, and there is less chance for them to carry forward bad habits.

One change can change many lives. When you give up smoking, you are improving your health, your relationships, and many other areas of your life. The compound effect of this change is enormous in your health and the people around you. You are doing a big favor not only for yourself but also for the lives of future generations.

Contents

Introduction

Well done is better than well said. Benjamin Franklin[1]

You have done the hardest part already. The rest is easy in comparison. You have a burning desire to quit, which means you are ready. There may be a few things that are pulling you back, but those are minute and mainly psychological.

You are likely here not because you don't know what to do but because you want to have that extra push to keep you off the edge and prevent you returning to smoking. Let me tell you that all of these suggestions are easy; the hardest part was for you to find relevant information, and you have already done that.

I smoked for twenty years. Before I gave up smoking, I was up to two packets a day, and the intake of nicotine was extremely high. Cigarettes were an integral part of my life. I didn't know how to do anything without smoking. I suffered a lot and thought that I could never have a healthy life, thinking that I might even die of lung cancer. That didn't deter me. Somehow, I always found a way to block those thoughts and carry on.

I tried all types of nicotine lozenges for almost a year, which led to other side effects. I tried patches for a while, used various nicotine replacement therapy medicines prescribed by doctors, and tried hypnotherapy. None of this worked for me. It's not that this wouldn't work for someone else. If others are like me, the pattern of thoughts is what made me want to keep coming back to cigarettes. I used the exact tools mentioned in this book to quit smoking within a few days and never felt like having a cigarette again. If I can do it, you can do it.

People will tell you they have tried all the different products, like patches, gums, inhalers, and so forth, and they never worked. On the other hand, some people may say that most products failed; however, nicotine patches worked, or gum worked, or they quit cold turkey. All of these examples may be correct; however, you went through more significant changes in your life. All this time you were trying, you were creating an intense desire to quit. It increased every time you were trying, until you said enough is enough and you were ready to make a change. It was not the product that made you come to this point. Your desire and intention moved you to this point. Instead of repeating the process from the beginning like me, with trial and error, you can use methods highlighted in this book, making it surprisingly easy to quit. This way you can get to your desire and intention straightaway and kick-start the healing process. The process highlighted in this book will not only help you eliminate your cigarette habits but also improve many parts of your life at the same time. In essence, it is mainly a mental game, and if you have reached this point, you have reached the psychological threshold. Now it's easy to change, as quitting is primarily a mental game.

Now what?

There are many ideas in this book, and understanding and acting on those will push you in the right direction. You are ready, but you will need to work on decision-making exercises. You will also need to learn how to stick to your decisions and stay positive. Bit by bit, it will become straightforward, and you will never look back again.

Please remember that it's easy to quit. Everyone can do it. However, once the novelty wears off, people tend to go back. This is because they haven't worked on how to deal with it and want to bridge the void they feel. Can you blame them? I don't think so. Years of emotional attachment may have resulted in this condition. It's your body and every cell tuned to a particular way of life every day. When you try to change that, your body will say, "Hang on a second. Something doesn't feel right; why are you not abusing me today?" Your body has been suppressing the chemicals to deal with poison, and when the poison does not flow in your body, you can feel the desire for nicotine and intense cravings to feel that void.

There is a lot of information on how to quit but no quality information on how to stay a nonsmoker and not to desire cigarettes. I struggled trying to find useful information on how to stay quit as my old mind patterns would trigger and give in to smoking many times after I quit. This book bridges that gap and provides the tools required to deal with nicotine addiction.

If you are at the end of your life due to smoking, do you wish that you didn't smoke, knowing what you are going to leave behind, like your loved ones? Think of all the happiness and the comfortable life you could have had, not to mention all the conversations and good times you missed as you skipped everything to smoke every fifteen minutes.

CHAPTER 1

What Is It Going to Cost You?

◆◆◆

*It's not whether you get knocked down, it's
whether you get up.* Vince Lombardi[1]

The cost may be your life or the quality of your life. Imagine not being able to run, do any physical activities, looking much older as a sign of slowly going toward your grave. Some of you may not have to imagine, as you may be living that life right now. You may still be able to improve the quality of your life, no matter which stage you are in, and enjoy the life you have left, which is always precious.

You know the consequences, and you know all the information about the health hazards of smoking. However, you have been suppressing all these signs and ignoring all the truths. It's time not to ignore the fact, stop making excuses, and start changing your smoking habits a small bit at a time.

If you don't smoke one, you are smoking one fewer. One fewer causes less damage. If quitting cold turkey is not your thing, perhaps have a small goal of reducing one or two for a few days. Giving up nighttime cigarettes is a good start, as you will be able to stay a nonsmoker for a long time until morning. Many apps will give you an indication of how long you have not been smoking and what health benefits you are getting. These apps can be beneficial to see how fast you are starting to heal. Some also have stats on how many people are dying every day from smoking.

I don't recommend prolonging nicotine addiction at all. However, we need to address nicotine addiction differently and work on the way you think. The way of thinking is what gives cigarettes such a high value, and way of thinking is a medicine to get rid of this addiction for good.

You can ignore the bad smell, bad taste, health warnings, and cancer probability and still smoke. The main thing that we will need to work on is your ability to ignore these warnings, the notion of it's not happening to me; it's never going to happen to me; one smoke does not cause harm; I had a bad day. These kinds of thoughts are holding you down. However, don't worry. Using the techniques in this book, we will eradicate the association for the long haul, not just temporarily, and you will be smoke-free in no time.

CHAPTER 2

Why Now Is the Best Time

◆ ◆

Go confidently in the direction of your dreams. Live the
life you have imagined. Henry David Thoreau[1]

Now is the best time to quit because it is the only real time, and everything else you think of is either in the past or in the future. Cigarette smoking affects and harms every organ of your body, causes many diseases, and diminishes life quality as health reduces.[2,3] Avoiding smoking immediately starts repairing your body and lowers the risk of smoke-related diseases, adding longevity to your life.[2,3]

The following are some statistics from the United States. Smoking causes more deaths each year in the United States than combined causes like human immunodeficiency virus (HIV), illegal drug use, alcohol use, motor vehicle injuries, and firearm-related incidents. Smoking causes about 90 percent of all lung cancer deaths.[2,3] More women die from lung cancer each year than from breast cancer. Smoking causes about 80 percent of all deaths from chronic obstructive pulmonary disease (COPD).[2]

Compared to nonsmokers, smokers are more likely to be subjected to an increase in the risk of coronary heart disease by two to four times,[2,7] increase chances of stroke by two to four times,[1] increase the chances of developing lung cancer by twenty-five times in men[2] and close to twenty-six times in women[2]. Smoking causes lung diseases like emphysema and chronic bronchitis.[2, 3] Smokers are up to thirteen times more likely to die from COPD than nonsmokers are.[2] Smoking can cause cancer almost anywhere in your body.[2, 3]

Smoking makes it harder for a woman to become pregnant, reduces fertility, and increases the risk of congenital disabilities and miscarriage. Smoking also affects your teeth and gums and can cause tooth loss.[2] Smoking can also increase the risk for cataracts and can even cause age-related macular degeneration. The risk of developing diabetes is 30 to 40 percent higher for active smokers than nonsmokers.[2, 3]

Quitting smoking for one year reduces the chances of a heart attack drastically;[3] the risk of stroke reduces to about that of a nonsmoker within two to five years.[3] Another benefit is that risks for cancers in the mouth, throat, esophagus, and bladder drop by half within five years[2] and risk of dying from lung cancer drops by half in ten years.[3]

Knowing all these risks and issues, do you think smoking is worth it? If you don't think more deeply about this, you may feel that it's OK to continue. You may think you will lose social contacts and have to give up the relaxation that smoking offers. You may also feel that you would rather enjoy life than be stressed. Fear may arise with all these thoughts. Please know that most of the ideas about continuing to smoking are created by the mind. The truth is you will be more relaxed when you don't smoke, and nonsmokers don't have stress related to smoking. Smoking causes more stress when the craving kicks in. You are less relaxed when you smoke. If you get cancer, there is typically no going back. Your life will quickly shatter before your eyes. Rather than enjoying your life, you will have to focus on treatments, if it's not too late. Please know that there is nothing more important than your health.

If you have been smoking for a long time, you are likely good at ignoring all these health hazards and saying one cigarette won't kill you. Because of the slow poisonous nature of smoking, you may think that you have forever to live and you won't get it today or anytime soon. You may say that a few won't hurt or that you'll quit eventually, and you may continue to smoke. Knowing all these risks and understanding and reminding yourself of them will help you be more conscious of what you are putting in your mouth. Every day remind yourself of the dangers and know in the back of your mind that the one cigarette you put in your mouth today may be the one that causes cancer. Every smoke is doing you damage. I can't stress enough that this kind of realization is what you need to bring into your mind every day. Every day that you don't smoke, remind yourself that you are getting healthier and you are recovering, reducing the risks of cancer immensely. You don't need cigarettes to fulfill you.

Please read along, and we will go through various steps that will help you prepare for your journey towards being a nonsmoker.

CHAPTER 3

Identify Anchors

The most courageous act is still to think for yourself. Aloud. Coco Chanel[1]

Have you ever encountered a time when smoking habits were directly reflected in what you were doing? Do you have the urge to smoke when you wake up? What about if you have the habit of drinking coffee in the morning? Do you get the urge then? To name a few scenarios, below are the times where triggers for smoking are likely to occur. For example, as soon as you wake up in the morning; while drinking coffee or tea; before catching a train or bus; before driving to work; before entering the work building; during a lunch break; after your lunch; before or after you have a meeting; just before going for a job interview; after work; before dinner; after dinner; before going to bed; when you are with your smoker friends or in a social situation. The patterns are unique to each person depending on the circumstances of their daily life. However, the traits of triggers are universal.

Have you noticed that if you have the habit of waking up early in the morning, then your body automatically wakes up at that time? There is a mind, and there is a body. The mind controls the body, and the body triggers the mind. With smoking, this is a disaster. How can we get out of this dilemma? Once you practice how to control the mind and its decision-making habits, you will be more equipped to deal with auto-body suggestions. In this context, auto-body suggestion is how your body craves nicotine and your brain starts getting a suggestion. When your body doesn't get Nicotine, you may get multiple thoughts or suggestions on how to satisfy this craving. This may occur at regular times when you used to smoke. This can feel like a losing battle at times. Thoughts like one more smoke won't hurt may occupy your thinking process.

Your body is like a car that has sensors while reversing. The sensors feed the information to the dashboard. Your body also has sensors like skin, eyes, nose, muscles, and so forth, which supply information to the brain. For a trained mind, once the information reaches the brain, then you have a choice to work out what you want to do with it. For an untrained mind, it means reactions. You can't control the sensation that you are receiving, but you can choose what to do with it and which experience you want to feel within yourself.

Identify all these patterns and note when they occur. It is essential because once you identify the trends, you can be conscious about them. All these anchors automatically trigger when the situation arises. To destroy the patterns, this is the first exercise you need to do. It will only take you a couple of minutes to identify these patterns. I suggest you take a few minutes of quiet time when there is no distraction and think about all these patterns you do daily. Note the thought process right now if you are smoking.

In the next exercise, we will look at how to remove negative associations and replace them with positive associations. Please be mindful, as this exercise is critical if you are serious about giving up smoking. Whether you are listening to this book or reading it, please take some time now to identify patterns and then come back for the next exercise.

CHAPTER 4

Good Image

All that we are is the result of what we have thought. Buddha[1]

In this chapter, we will create a healthier image of yourself. To begin, let us ponder the following questions for a moment. Is there a time when you could think of yourself as an unbeatable, robust, and confident person? How did you feel when you were at the peak of your success? Please don't tell me you don't have any success with anything in your life. Success can be anything. Below are a few scenarios that will help you identify this state.

Consider the times in your life when you achieved something important to you. It could be your first job interview. It could be the first goal you scored in a football game. It could be your first date, when you were successful in finding your loved one. Your first baby. The first time you made someone happy by helping with something. The time when you felt great when you helped the poor. The time when you were so confident that no one or nothing could stop you from achieving what you set your mind out to do. It is any right time that you can tap. Once you find a healthier image of yourself, you need to create a healthier picture of yourself. This image needs to be brighter, healthier, stronger, and confident. This image is something you want to feel after quitting smoking.

In a moment, I will ask you to close your eyes and create an image in your mind. It can be anything, like obtaining a six-pack, a muscular body, or curves. You can personalize as you wish. Again, note that it can be anything. Take this image based on your previous experience and add to it. A healthier you will stand straighter with a smile, not be afraid of your breath, and will be able to be active and look good in the clothes you are wearing.

An image for a nonsmoker can be a person who can breathe easily, has no issues running, has lots of confidence, and has skin that looks amazing, and feels livelier because clean blood is flowing in all parts of the body. This is the image of a person who is not afraid to challenge himself or herself. Now you can place this image in your favorite places. Placing the image is not physical; it's the imagination alone. As an example, I always picture myself in one of the islands of Fiji, next to clear blue water. This place always makes me happy, and your image needs to do the same, which is to make yourself feel pleasant and relaxed. Now close your eyes for two minutes and create this image.

If you can hold this positive thought in your mind for more than one minute, then you can have a compound effect that will start the momentum toward a healthier you straightaway. The right image is the one you want to refer to every time you feel stressed; the idea is that when you think about this image, you feel happy. It may take a little bit of time to get used to this exercise; however, the more you practice, the better you will become at it. In the beginning, you may forget to do it, maybe causing you stress already. Or nothing happens when you start thinking of your image, as there is a tug-of-war going on in your mind between pulling you toward smoking and trying to feel relaxed at the same time. Keep practicing and this exercise alone will be your go-to place, which will help you immensely.

Make this image as vivid as possible. If you could go back in time when you were not smoking, add that image as well. The whole idea of this is to create a picture that gives you a perfect vibe. Whenever you can see this image in an internal projector of your mind, you should see an instant change in your perception. Please keep on practicing until this image becomes second nature. In the coming chapters, this image will be critical, and we will use this image to replace bad habits.

Create three to four good images that you can refer to easily; this can also be situation related. Some suggestions are that maybe you felt perfect when you were playing with your kids; perhaps the vivid image of the last holiday you took is one that makes you feel terrific. It may be some particular scenery or one specific situation that makes you feel good every time you look at that image through your mind's eye. You need to create a few of these images so you can access them easily.

I also created the image of the local pond where I usually see many ducks. I took my kids there, and I remember feeling blessed and happy. The view touches my heart, with its beautiful water, fantastic mild sunrays shining on the water, and a gentle breeze caressing the skin. I picture this image every time I am stressed, and it gives me a sense of peace straightaway.

CHAPTER 5

Choose a Quit Date

The future starts today, not tomorrow. Pope John Paul II[1]

Choose a date when you would like to stop smoking. You need to pick a time that suits you the best. Do not try to quit when you have a heavy work schedule if that's when you usually smoke. For those who work Monday through Friday, many may find it more manageable by choosing a Friday rather than a Monday. A long weekend is another good time. It's not that you can't do it on a Monday. It's just that you generally relax more on the weekends and have more options and tools to keep yourself calm and relaxed.

Choosing a quit date sets the tone for the new journey on which you are embarking. Our minds always try to restart and set goals with the start of the new week, new month, new year, and so forth. In this scenario, quitting on Friday tricks your mind into thinking that you have achieved a lot of progress toward your new week. If you quit at 8pm on Friday and wake up at 6am on Saturday, you have already been smoke-free for up to ten hours. Having a few days off and preparing yourself gives you a stronger mindset. Remember, quitting smoking can be easy, and mindset is most of it. Why is all of this important? It's because you can give yourself all the necessary tools and sound knowledge to tackle your mind's and body's habits.

Selecting a specific date is another form of making decisions. Once you decide on a quit date and stick to it, things will automatically start to look different. Your single committed, decisive action has such a profound impact that the whole universe will line up for you to succeed. This decision needs to be made from the right place, however. If you decide out of desperation, then most likely you will continue toward the same despair. Understand that with smoking, there is nothing to gain and possibly everything to lose. Make this decision with full consciousness.

Once you make a decision, you need to follow through, as your life depends on it. And that one decision means you will achieve all the goals and much more. You are making the decision not only to reach your goal but also becoming the kind of person who can achieve the goals. In the next chapter, we will do an exercise to remove negative associations as far as the habit of smoking.

CHAPTER 6

Diminish Anchors

Little by little, one travels far. J.R.R. Tolkien[1]

In previous chapters, we identified anchors that trigger auto responses toward smoking. In this chapter, we will replace anchors with an image that you created previously. If you are a heavy smoker, then you have created many anchors. We don't want to change all of them at once, and we should only pick a few of them and then replace them gradually. Replacing a few anchors first is the key to success. Once you are done with a few, replacing others will be easy. Let's consider an example. When you wake up, you get the urge to smoke. You always give in and smoke as soon as that trigger is set. On the quit date, I want you to do what follows repeatedly.

When you get this feeling to smoke, acknowledge it. Then picture yourself smoking cigarettes in your usual place when you wake up. Now make that image black and white in your head. Every time you see this image, replace it with the feel-good image that you have created in previous chapters.

Anthony Robbins. (2003) has shown the slingshot mechanism to diminish anchors[11]. This method requires more imagination. Put your bad image in front of your eyes. Now put a feel-good image in a slingshot, stretch it hard, and let it go. Picture a feel-good image getting bigger and bigger, coming toward your eyes and breaking the black-and-white image. Do this about sixty times every time you see your smoking image picture. The slingshot of feel-good image comes and brings the bad one down or breaks it every time you feel an urge. This is one method for replacing your anchors. Use all of your senses when you are practicing. Replace one anchor at a time and envision the image broken into small pieces and vanishing. Keep practicing and you should feel incredible as soon as you wake up in the morning, rather than feel an urge to smoke. This exercise is a significant step toward your success, which will allow you to replace a negative anchor. Of course, your brain will try to fight it by saying one more is OK and you can't function without smoking—that you are stressed, enjoy smoking, and so forth. The main action you need to take is acknowledging the feeling and saying you are not that image anymore for that particular anchor.

This step starts your healing process immediately. When your brain knows that you are giving up smoking, many feelings will continue. Overcoming this is a key. Once you can replace one anchor, pat yourself on the back, as you have achieved a significant milestone. This milestone will massively encourage you and will be critical to your success.

Now gradually do this to all anchors within a few days. Keep practicing and you will get better at it. You can't avoid the surroundings, but you can change the surroundings in your mind. Instead of blaming the environment, people, and situations, change how you think. How it occurs to you is unique to you, and you will have total control over it.

Conditioning is the key to success. When you feel like smoking, find healthier alternatives to change what occurs in your surroundings. Don't rush this process. You are quitting for the long haul. Each anchor that you have created makes you smoke. Therefore, it's ideal to replace all the anchors slowly and effectively.

CHAPTER 7

Apply Substitute Only When Needed

You have power over your mind – not outside events. Realize this, and you will find strength. Marcus Aurelius[1]

We want to avoid any substitute options as much as possible. However, substitutes can be useful in some instances. If you are unsure, please consult your health-care professionals if you have a situation that needs attention.

As soon as you tell your brain that you are changing something, your mind fights back and informs the body to do the same. You were born with this instinct, as your brain wants to make you more comfortable all the time. The brain's response to your change is to ask why you want to change something that has been with you all this time. You will become stressed. You might think there's so much pleasure in smoking. Only today. Only this packet of cigarettes. I'll quit on a sunny day when I don't have to deal with everyday life. I'll stop when I have a long holiday. Only one more cigarette. The brain is disguising the small itch of cravings and making them into gigantic ones, repeating them back to you and making them worse.

To deal with this in early stages, if it's necessary, you may want to look at nicotine replacement therapy after consulting a doctor. However, as I said, I recommend going without any of these substitutes if possible. You can choose to try healthy substitutions like munching carrots and exercising instead of using nicotine. The idea is that you don't give any excuses to your brain and deal with the body's reaction to some deprivation of nicotine. Please bear in mind that no substitute in this world works if you are not ready. It's *you* who needs to make this conscious decision, and it's *you* who gives up smoking, not any replacement therapy. I have seen many people who do this substitute therapy consistently fail. The reason may be their untrained minds. I battled tremendously due to this. I was addicted to nicotine lozenges for almost two years. I developed a fear of nicotine lozenges running out and used to carry multiple boxes with me. I would pop these in my mouth even if I didn't have any urge for nicotine, just because I started feeling good and felt less agitation. I developed severe anxiety about losing a calm state, so I kept taking those nicotine tablets.

It's essential to train your brain. You don't have to substitute with something physical; you can replace the habit with something mental. You can't change the occurrence, but you can change how it affects you. In previous chapters, you have identified the times when you smoke. Focus on getting pleasure in different ways—listening to music, having a conversation with loved ones, changing the route to avoid the place where you usually smoke—so you are in the new environment. Together with removing anchor ideas, you can visit those old places with new meaning once your mind and thoughts are more stable. The plan is to practice soon and often. Replace the old image with a new one when you visit the old place.

Every accomplishment is something to treasure. Don't have big goals; have small ones and be successful at it first. For example, if you have stopped one occurrence in a day when you usually smoke, that's a victory.

Don't be disheartened or feel guilty if you slip. Know that you are in progress and that the ideas highlighted in previous chapters will slowly and surely replace your old habits with new ones—for good. Keep moving and restart.

CHAPTER 8

Tell Everyone

The journey of a thousand miles begins with one step. Lao Tzu[1]

If you are a person who achieves success when you tell people that you have committed, then be sure to tell people so they can support you, whether your son/daughter, your spouse, your circle of friends, and so on.

People around will support you in this transition. You may feel that you don't want to let people down, which may give you enough energy to quit or practice mental exercises.

In many cases, your environment does not change when you want to change. Therefore, you will get constant trigger points to remind you to smoke. You may be in social situations where you get regular triggers, especially in a condition where all the family members smoke. Telling everyone can relieve some pressure, as friends and family members will usually respect and support your choice to regain your health. If the environment is hostile, using some substitute beforehand may be a good idea; your essential goal, which is not to smoke, remains intact.

It depends on your target goal. A substitute like nicotine lozenges keeps the momentum going. However, it can make it difficult for you to get rid of the addiction to nicotine itself. While I recommend that you do without a substitute, as you don't need it, I also know that years of conditioning insofar as environmental stimulation will trigger your desire to smoke. It gives you that extra time to strengthen your mindset. Every time you avoid in the same environment/situation is a victory. It all depends on how healthy your mindset is already. If you can cope and say no straightaway, this is ideal. If not, try to avoid it. If you can't, then do mind exercises beforehand. Don't plan to fail but have a plan to succeed.

In addition, telling everyone makes you accountable. When you are responsible, you will put in extra effort not to let others down. When you are going to the gym by yourself, do you sometimes lose motivation and feel like not going on that day? If your answer is no, then you are much stronger mentally than you think you are and giving up smoking will be easier for you. However, if your answer is yes, you are at the other end of the spectrum, which means you will genuinely benefit from your accountability partner. Some people can let themselves down, but not others, which means letting other people down is not part of their belief system. If you know that your gym buddy is going to be waiting for you, then you will make every effort to go there. In many cases, accountability partners take you out of your comfort zone and make you accountable for your actions. Once you are responsible for your actions, you can become whatever/whoever you'd like to be.

Another reason to tell your loved ones is because they will be able to tolerate you during this process. Without realizing it, you may say or act in a way that hurts people, usually your loved ones, and they become your emotional punching bag. There is no excuse to behave in the wrong way; however, when you tell your loved ones, they may be able to direct their responses in a way where you may not react. The agitated state is the cause of many issues, and the last thing you want is your family to respond in the same way due to your heightened agitation. You may not know or may not have realized it, but you have been putting your family through a lot with your smoking habits. Your family has probably been nothing but supportive of you this whole time. Don't make it hard on them by not telling anyone. They won't know why you are acting the way you are. Let your loved ones know and they will typically support you even more.

Remember, it's your issue, not the problem of people around you. When you fix this issue, you will benefit, which in turn makes you feel better with the people around you and causes you to react pleasantly. People will like you because you are pleasant to be around, and the cycle will continue.

CHAPTER 9

Find Healthy Habits

*If you think you can do a thing or think you can't
do a thing, you're right. Henry Ford[1]*

Finding healthy habits is an essential part of your goal. It gives you an extra push to continue your path and makes your mind more in control. Healthy habits include exercise, drinking plenty of water throughout the day, going for a walk when you usually smoke, watching related motivational videos, yoga, practicing meditation, and so forth.

A study conducted by Stanford[10] has found that spending time in nature can reduce the risk of depression. The published study found that people walking for ninety minutes in a natural environment as opposed to high traffic urban areas showed decreased activity in a region of the brain associated with depression.

These habits not only help you divert your mind but also help you recover faster. When you start healthy habits at the same time, you are quickly moving towards a new image of yourself. You are removing bad smoking habits and adding new ones. You are becoming stronger, and your ability to breathe is getting better. Your mind is getting much stronger, and many other improvements are happening to you. These recovery actions will determine how successful you are going to be in all facets of your life. Many things in your life can hold you up, and they may be related to the same hurdle you are trying to overcome. By removing one, you may open many new possibilities. Your sense of achievement and overcoming will help you in many areas of your life. Things you have been putting off may finally start to get some traction.

Healthy habits move you towards a new way of life. Please exercise and find other healthy habits you can do immediately. Daily physical activity is an excellent way to improve your health straightaway. At first, you may find it difficult, so I recommend taking small steps. Just go for a walk in the morning as soon as you wake up and listen to positive music and audiobooks, watch inspiring videos, and so on. Mainly concentrate on the benefits you are getting as soon as you achieved being smoke-free. The idea is to improve your health straightaway so your recovery is much faster, and positive thinking will get the momentum going.

CHAPTER 10

Stay Positive

You only live once, but if you do it right, once is enough. Mae West[1]

Healthy habits don't have to be just physical. They can be mental as well. They both go hand in hand. Thinking positively throughout the day will make you automatically refrain from smoking once you quit. When you have healthy thoughts, it's hard for your body to be unhealthy. You would have to try to force yourself into bad habits. In the early stage of being smoke-free, it's easier to have negative thoughts. Every time you do, immediately catch yourself and say it is just a thought and that now you want to think good thoughts. It can start with the following:

> I felt so good this morning when I had a coffee.
> It's a beautiful day.
> I am breathing beautiful and clean air, which feels so
>   much better.
> I had a pleasant time with my kids yesterday.
> I accomplished many tasks yesterday.
> I am grateful for my eyes, nose, ear, and so forth.
> My body knows how to heal itself.

> Healthy cells are vibrating in my body.
> My body is cleaning itself.

The idea is to move towards positivity and towards appreciating your health slowly. It would be hard to move from negative thoughts to positive thoughts immediately, so the small transition is essential. Please make a list of ten things that can make you feel good and write them down. This way you have lists that you can refer to multiple times a day to be in a good mood. You can do this in every situation.

For example, suppose you are angry at someone, let's say Amy, your wife. Instead of thinking about how upset you are with Amy, you can think something like, *Amy can be annoying sometimes, but not all the time. Amy makes me angry sometimes, but not always. When Amy is not in this mood, we like each other's company. Last time I had lunch with her, we had a perfect time. The food was delicious. She made a joke that I liked.* Negative thoughts may come again, like, *I don't want to think good about her because I'm still angry.*

You can acknowledge thoughts as thoughts only, and this has no power over you. Say thank you for making me aware of this thought and again start thinking positive things about Amy or an entirely different subject so you can feel better first and deal with the situation. By the time you finish this exercise, you will feel much better, and if Amy did the same, that would be even better. If Amy is still upset, then at least you are not angry and can deal with it in a much better fashion.

CHAPTER 11

Accept Healing Consciously

It does not matter how slowly you go so long as you do not stop. Confucius[1]

Positive thought has a lot more power than we can probably comprehend. When you replace negative thoughts with positive ones, your whole perspective and environment can change. Instead of saying, "I am quitting cigarettes," you may want to focus on getting healthier. Every time you don't smoke, think that you don't need nasty toxins in your body. You are getting stronger every single minute. With every heartbeat, you can picture clean oxygen pumped throughout your body, repairing all damaged cells and leaving you feeling energised.

The simple fact is that negative thoughts move you towards negative behaviour, and positive ones move you towards positive behaviour. The feel-good thoughts are your secret shifters, and these thoughts will ensure that you are favorable throughout the day. If negative thoughts enter your mind, acknowledge them and deliberately focus on things that make you feel good. You may feel good about past experiences where you were in control or times when you were feeling good. These are the times you want to have it in your memory on an as-need basis. You may have pictures of the past that remind you of a good time. You can add such pictures as a bookmark or an easily accessible place so you can refer to it as you need it and deliberately focus on it to change your thoughts.

Your feelings are the guide. If you can feel positive emotions in your body, then you can be sure that you are having positive thoughts at this point. Taking a deep breath a few times and concentrating on good memory will start firing feel-good chemicals in your body. Healing occurs when you accept the current moment and acknowledge something about which you are grateful. If you are thankful for small things, you will receive your heart's desires in no time.

CHAPTER 12

Have Only One Goal at a Time

◆◆◆

By failing to prepare, you are preparing to fail. Benjamin Franklin[1]

When you have a goal to give up smoking and live a healthy life, you want to focus on that goal for a specified period. The human brain sometimes wants to achieve many desires when it feels we are in the rhythm of success. You may have goals to eat healthily, start physical activities, improve your work situation, improve your personal life, deliver successful projects, achieve wealth, or what have you. All of those are great, but this time consider focusing on one primary goal, which is to be smoke-free. Reaching this one goal does not affect only one part of your life; it affects multiple. When you stop smoking, you immediately stop taking the toxins into your body and start repairing it. You move towards a healthy body, and you will remove the bondage from nicotine addiction, clearing your mind and building your confidence. This one area of your life is the cause of most of your problems. One pattern of blockage is running almost all parts of your life. Break this bad habit and you'll have the freedom to achieve your desired experiences.

Having too many clusters of thoughts and patterns in your mind will move you away from achieving the first goal itself. Often, one bad habit is everywhere. You may realize that one habit is responsible for making you feel awful. If your goal is to focus on being healthy and quit smoking, then make that goal a priority. Everything else can wait. I know some of us are either all or nothing. While the quitting smoking momentum is going for a few days, you may feel like adding more things on your plate. It may be something like reading more books and working on a project you have been putting off for a long time. I know it's tempting to start on something else immediately after some success, but please hold off on anything else until you have quit smoking for good. You may do meditation and so forth to quiet your mind in the morning, but it should be all related to your primary goal.

One bad habit may be stopping you from going to the gym. It may be the same reason you don't want to split household chores or be a good parent, as you are busy smoking every opportunity you get. You may be procrastinating because you are still thinking of smoking. Change this one habit and you will unlock the potential to achieve much more than one thing at the same time.

CHAPTER 13

Practice Every Day

I fear not the man who has practiced 10,000 kicks once, but I fear the man who has practiced one kick 10,000 times. Bruce Lee[1]

It's ideal that you practice thinking positive every day. Remind yourself every single day about achievements so far, what you are gaining, and take a note of your health benefits.

You will want to read quotes that empower you when the craving kicks in. Nicotine withdrawal that you are experiencing is slight and subtle, and your body has enough tools to deal with it. The void that you are experiencing is mental, so you must remind yourself that you are not giving up anything useful.

Practicing every day with affirmations creates a rhythm. It will build your belief system, and you will no longer think about smoking in the same way. Even if you get five minutes of free time in a day, that would be enough to move in the right direction. Ideally, practice positive thinking throughout your day, such as one minute every hour, or you may choose to do so at certain times during the day, like in the morning, lunchtime, during bathroom breaks, late lunch, evening, nighttime.

This simple habit will help you move in the right direction. When you boil water, it takes the right amount of energy to convert water into vapor. Once it has, it has changed state. Practicing every day is like heating water. After twenty to thirty days, you won't be the same person anymore. You will have changed like vapor, still water but in a different state. When you have new conditioning, you won't do the things you used to do, as your further success will compound and attract other changes. For people who are skeptical about making this change immediately, please know that this is a healthy change and embrace it as if your life depends on it.

CHAPTER 14

Be Present

◆◆◆

The unexamined life is not worth living. Socrates[1]

When you are in a stressful situation, it's easier to lose present mode. Then your subconscious mind may go on autopilot, which can trigger urges to smoke. It's ideal to remind yourself to be present. When thoughts come into your mind, intercept immediately, acknowledging and removing all the stories that are associated with it. If you get urges to smoke, think about the toxins that would go into your body. Affirm to yourself that you will not even take one puff—no more cigarettes.

Stories have many layers, and when you are present, you can see things as they are rather than attaching years of beliefs and many of your stories. When you are seeing things through the foggy glass for a long time, you believe that's your reality and you forget the last time you were able to see clearly. When you remove layers/stories out of the situation, all you see is the situation. It's easy to deal with situations. Examples of stories are nothing will happen if I have one more. I can always quit later. I like going to sleep late and waking up late; the last time I woke up early, I felt miserable; I love a warm bed; I don't want to feel rushed; I want to only care about what I feel now rather than later.

Removing layers is tricky, but once you get the hang of it, it gives you so much clarity that you will question why you didn't do this earlier. Try to see everything as is. See smoking as it is rather than with any layers of benefit or pleasure you may have added. If you want to do a quick experiment to see without layers, inhale a few puffs of smoke and feel the taste and smell. Does it feel awful? That's what smoke tastes like in real life. But when you say that smoking makes you feel good, gives you pleasure, removes stress and you also associate times when you felt great, then you do not see it as is but through layers. That's all the conditioning that you have attached to smoking. Moreover, the feel-good feeling you get is because of addictive nicotine. However, the nicotine craving part is so small that you can barely feel it. When there are multiple layers, the craving becomes big.

In the book *The How of Happiness*, Sonia Lyubomirsky, a leading researcher, highlighted that we control up to 40 percent of our potential happiness.[8] Out of the 60 percent remaining, 50 percent of our happiness is predetermined at birth and 10 percent is dictated by circumstances.[8] This study illustrates that it's not merely genes we inherit that determine our destinies but that we are in charge of a significant chunk of our lives.

Another way to be present is by focusing on breathing and noting how your body feels when you are inhaling and exhaling. When thoughts arise, pay attention to them. Be mindful of how everything feels. If you are washing your hands, feel the water and notice the feeling. If you are eating, explore the food and identify what kind of taste it has. The more you become present, the less you will let your mind go on autopilot mode, which will help you stay on your path for success.

CHAPTER 15

You Can't Always Change Circumstances, but You Can Change What Occurs

Whatever you are, be a good one. Abraham Lincoln[1]

When you change, the circumstances do not change, but with your mind, you can change what occurs. When something happens in your life, you can change how it affects you.

To give you an example, your spouse may have the habit of complaining. When you finish your work and reach home, you may have preoccupied thoughts that might lead to your spouse complaining. Even if your spouse isn't complaining, you will automatically react as if he or she did. Instead, you could change that action to being thankful for your spouse for letting you know what happened during the day, about finances, kids, about their work. Change complaining into the information being supplied to you and appreciate it.

When you start doing this, you will instantly take the focus out of negative and lean towards positive change. This action will have a significant effect on your life and will improve all areas of your life immediately.

Thinking there may be other aspects and changing the exercise will help you deal with a void or emptiness after you quit smoking.

When things happen, try not to associate any stories with it. Remove all the layers and try to see things for as they are. If you feel stressed, it is just your physical sensation and not because you may not like your mother-in-law, as an example. We give so many layers to the situation and things in our life that we sometimes can't distinguish what is real and what's not. Remove all the layers and you can deal with the situations more easily.

You have minimal control over your surroundings and environments, and they are not going to change to appeal to your wishes. The only way to achieve what you want is to change yourself. Your inner world governs the external world. You, and only you, are in control of the inner world, and no one but you should determine what happens there.

CHAPTER 16

Beat Cravings

Love all, trust a few, do wrong to none. William Shakespeare[1]

When cravings occur, treat them as they are. They are cravings, nothing else. Note that it is not craving smoke but the craving of nicotine that causes withdrawals. When you remove any association of withdrawal with smoking, it becomes easy to deal with cravings. These cravings will feel like thirst or hunger and will feel very subtle. You deal with many complicated body feelings every day, and this withdrawal craving will be minute in comparison. If you divert your mind to something else, you will quickly forget this craving. It can be anything, like listening to your favorite music, watching favorite shows, and so forth.

You can play games or go for a walk. Cravings will only last for a few seconds to a few minutes. The more you don't put the focus on the desire and smoking part, the better you can faster beat the cravings.

You can also create in your mind a secret place. This mysterious place has a door, and once you open the door, you are in a different world. Only you have access to this door, and you control what's inside this door. This place consists of only happy parts of your life, and everything is magical here. You can be whatever you want, eat whatever your heart desires, and bring any of your loved ones. When you are in this place, you should feel happy, so feel free to get serious in your imagination. This place can also be from previous times you have visited, when you had the perfect experience. Turn that memory into a magical memory. Add all the things that you've wanted in your life. Every time you have cravings, you can go to this place and relax.

CHAPTER 17

Clear Limiting Beliefs

The path to success is to take massive, determined action. Tony Robbins[1]

"I can never give up smoking, and I won't be able to function without it." Does that sound familiar? Limiting beliefs limit us from doing many things, and we may not realize why we do certain things the way we do. One of the best ways to get rid of limiting beliefs is with affirmations. Although affirmations may not sound real at first, they do make you focus on things that you are trying to accomplish. By practicing daily, you could rewire your internal neuro systems and reprogram your mind. Affirmations have a profound impact on my life, and I highly recommend you use them to clear your limiting beliefs. Limiting beliefs are like a rule book or a law book. You use this rule book to make any future decisions. If your rule book is wrong or corrupted, your choices will be wrong too and your life can move in a different direction than intended.

Many times we don't know what makes us stop doing things and why we are self-sabotaging the outcome. The answer may lie deep in your belief system, and it may be from your childhood. You can think about it and try to unravel it. However, it's necessary to do affirmations. You can start with simple ones and start connecting to what you are affirming with all your senses. You can clear your limiting belief by creating a belief system that is stronger than what you have currently.

Try to change very simple beliefs first and work your way through. Here is a straightforward example that I tried with my children. My son Noah didn't think he was good at catching a ball, so for a long time, he didn't even want to try it. His brother, Ilias, however, is very good at playing the catch game. Noah's belief system led him to be fearful of dropping it. When he noticed that he was not nearly as good as his brother, he didn't want to play the game, but he continued because I was enthusiastic about it. He would flinch and close his eyes every time I passed him the ball. So, I did a small experiment to work on his belief system. I brought both kids close to me and then tossed the ball one at a time to each kid. As Noah caught the ball, I said to him, "Look how good you are." I also told that him he was as good as his brother was. I praised them both. Noah gave a small smile, and I noticed that his whole persona changed. Every time they caught the ball successfully, I asked them to move one step back. I praised them every time. Soon he was catching it from far away. This was the first time Noah was not scared to catch the ball from such a distance, and he didn't miss a single one. You can use this example and try it in any scenario in your life.

If you are struggling with the pattern of self-sabotage and are not able to help yourself when you need to, then your limiting belief may be sabotaging your progress. When you see that you are starting to improve, your limiting belief may prevent you from pursuing further improvements. Limiting belief is the one that causes life to be less than completely satisfying. These beliefs can be something like I can never give up smoking; I fail at discipline; I have a weak brain; I can't control my thoughts. Investing some time and exploring limiting beliefs may be one of the best things you can do in your life. Limiting beliefs are like wearing foggy glasses. Everything you see through those glasses keeps you stuck in life-limiting thoughts and patterns.

To heal, we need to work out what kind of limiting belief it is. There may be different types of limiting beliefs that can initiate from not feeling safe, not feeling deserving, feeling you can't do certain things, or staying as you are because you think it's benefiting you. For example, you may feel you get attention when you are sick, which may be the reason you are not able to heal.

The trick to clearing limiting beliefs is to acknowledge that you have such beliefs in the first place, believing that this is not serving you well and it's time to change and that it's safe to do so. You need to find or create a powerful empowering belief to replace the old ones.

CHAPTER 18

Practice Approximately Sixty Times a Day

I came, I saw, I conquered. Julius Caesar[1]

Why practice sixty times a day? Practicing many times a day will reinforce the image you have created and remind yourself as many times as possible. You can choose to do more or a bit less. I did find that doing it approximately sixty times or more helped me immensely on that day. I believe this is the fastest way to reprogram your mind, which usually takes a long time. If you don't practice, it's easy to fall back into automatic mind patterns quickly, which will trigger cravings. If you do not identify the craving's nature, you may give in easily.

One of the techniques that you could use in the early stage after quitting is to associate everyday items or processes to the image. Map the typical journey you do every day in your brain and know your route. For instance, you wake up, use the bathroom, take a shower, put work clothes on, sit down for breakfast, open the front door, drive or walk or catch a bus, reach work, enter through the door of your office, and go to your desk. You will notice that there is a common area or things that you encounter multiple times, like the door. Now associate your image of success with the door. Every time you go through a door, remind yourself about your feel-good image. Remind yourself at every traffic light where you're stopped.

All of these hacks are for the initial phase only. After practicing and repeating, you will condition yourself to see the new picture and diminish the old you. To remind yourself, you could even set alarms that go off every hour. I use an alarm on my watch that vibrates every hour. You can also listen to your favorite music every few hours. When choosing to play music, ensure that you are playing something positive that makes you feel good.

This idea is to keep feeling wonderful multiple times a day. When you feel good, it's easy to reinforce what you are becoming, how healthy you feel, how much you are enjoying being smoke-free.

CHAPTER 19

Create Your Conditioning

◆◆◆

You miss 100 percent of the shots you never take. Wayne Gretzky[1]

You need to do two types of conditioning. I want to term these as downhill and uphill conditioning. Let's first go to downhill conditioning. You need to associate all the bad things about smoking in this exercise. Imagine that you just put a cigarette in your mouth and took a puff. Straightaway imagine the taste of a toilet or dead mouse in your mouth. You should feel disgusted. Inhale one more mouthful. Feel the taste of a repulsive smell like vomit or diarrhea. If that's not strong enough, feel it in your mouth. Make it disgusting.

Repeat this in your brain forty times.

If this is your first day of quitting, you can do this every hour. It rewrites your subconscious mind for auto responses. After practicing this, you won't be able to picture pleasure with smoking. You may gag at the thought of taking one puff. On the other hand, you may feel good about not smoking. I am excited for you to try this.

Uphill conditioning is the opposite of downhill conditioning. You will associate all the positive aspects rather than the negative ones. Positive thoughts are like health benefits, repairing lungs and moving you to your healthy image. Every hour make yourself feel as if you are at the top of the world. You can relate to pleasing times you had in the past when you were not smoking. Do this forty times after downhill conditioning.

Uphill conditioning is like a reward system. Every time you do well, you reward yourself with happy feelings. You should soon start feeling bad about smoking and enjoyable for not smoking.

CHAPTER 20

Practicing Your Muscles

Life is either a daring adventure or nothing at all. Helen Keller[1]

To build muscles, you need to exercise regularly. You need to train your brain muscles regularly to stop smoking as well. In the beginning, practice by saying no to things other than smoking. For example, say no to drinking soft drinks or eating junk food, whatever you crave. It varies from person to person. Your brain will probably come up with many reasons for you to change the decision. What you feel is going to go away soon. You need to wait it out.

Every person is unique, and the reasons will be different for each person. Merely practicing resisting the urges will take you closer to your result. You are trying to counterattack the mind-made bad suggestions with positive ones. You're practicing the muscles of your brain. Come up with ten reasons that you should avoid smoking and reflect on them as often as you can. Practice a minimum of ten times a day. This practice takes only a few seconds. However, those few seconds will save your life. If you run out of things to practice, make up a hypothetical scenario about things you love.

For example, let's say you have low resistance when you see chocolate. If you pretend that it is in front of you and you are putting it away by saying no, you will need reasons to say no. Your brain will come up with all the ideas as to why you should go ahead with that chocolate. You can apply the same approach in the case of smoking. This strategy works very well to avoid smoking. Remember one lousy habit carried out throughout your life and fix that one bad habit to improve your life experience drastically. That pattern applies to other areas of life. Practice this for a few days and observe the changes in your mind. You are not only impacting the habit; you are changing your mindset completely.

CHAPTER 21

Aftermath

Better to build a bridge than a wall. Elton John[1]

It is normal to feel a void once you quit smoking. You may also miss it and keep pondering what it's like to smoke. Acting appropriately at this time is crucial. This is when you will need to make your brain strong. When you get this feeling, you will need to practice positive image exercise. When you feel some void, it is best to go internal and find out where this feeling is coming from, what it looks like, which area of your body you are feeling this in. Take a few long breaths and try to identify the void. Does it feel like small hunger pangs, perhaps, rather than smoke cravings? By the time you complete the exercise, the void may go away. You need to wait it out a few minutes and it will go. Soon this space will become smaller and smaller and you will be able to deal with the void instantly. Drinking a glass of water at that moment may help you immensely.

When you get this feeling, what you do within the next few seconds will lead you towards success or failure. All the work you have done so far boils down to these small moments. The more you practice and deal with not having a cigarette, the stronger your dealings will be. As mentioned earlier, this feeling may also feel similar to the hunger feeling, with the brain deceiving you into making this more significant than it is. If your mind says, *I need one right now*, your practice should enable you to say you *don't* need one right now. You should know that having one will remove all the effort you've done; it will start addiction all over again. You don't want that. If you need to find anything outside yourself during the early days, carrots and celery sticks may help distract you for those few seconds. Remember, even one smoke can kill you. Think about the good times you had in your life, and the symptoms will pass away shortly.

Everything starts with a thought, and if you quit, it's mainly due to your thought. If you don't, that is also because of your thought. Once you take responsibility for your actions, you will understand that you had the choice all the time. Sometimes it probably felt as if the environment was influencing you to smoke; in reality, you made that choice. Since you made that choice, you can easily make another choice. At first, it may look like an impossible task, but if you don't do it right now, you can fall into the same trap. It may not be easy, but it's not hard either. Don't doubt your decisions about quitting, and remember that you are doing a favor for yourself, your family, and entire new generations.

This process is an essential part of this whole process. What you do at this step of your quitting journey will determine your success or failure. Remember, if you fall to one, you will keep on falling. If you need more support from your surroundings for a few days, this is the time to reach out. It is so easy to fall in this stage, as the mind wants to give up. On the second or third day, your mind may say to have one. You need to be very firm and say no and move on. Remember, you have decided to quit; stick to your decision. If you can say no without the feeling of missing out, it means that you have practiced appropriately. After this step, your journey gets better and better. After a week, you may be in the same position, so please do the same thing.

Your body is a fantastic machine and is extremely smart. Each part of the body can learn individually. Now that you don't smoke, what will you do when your body triggers cravings that used to cause you to smoke? Your body will trigger sensation, and in turn, your mind is going to treat it as the need for a smoke. If you understand that it is just an addiction and utilize the teaching you learned in previous steps, you can easily defeat your inner thoughts.

When the trigger happens, here is an example of what you might be able to do. Your mind thinks of wanting a cigarette. You can acknowledge it and think of how long you have been smoke-free, how clean your blood has been. Last time the same trigger happened, the best decision you made was not to give in. You have been healthy since. You don't want to give all that away. All the repair work that your body has done shouldn't be going to waste. Imagine taking in fresh air. Feel how easy it is to breathe. Appreciate the amazing gift that you have. The idea is to acknowledge first, think about all the benefits, and be thankful.

Do some gratitude exercises. For example: I am so thankful for my life. I can enjoy my life without toxins in my body. Each cell in my body is thanking me. I am getting attractive and amazing. I am thankful for everything around me. We should practice gratitude regularly. Gratitude is very powerful and helps get rid of negative emotions quickly. Robert Emmons, one of the leading gratitude researchers, demonstrated that regular gratitude reduced the feeling of envy and resentment.[9] With regular practice, you will soon be able to get rid of all negative thoughts and emotions that you used to feel. In my experience, gratitude is a swift way of healing your life. I practice gratitude every morning and always write down five things that I am grateful for in my journal. Once I finish writing this list, I usually go back and try to feel the gratitude with all my senses, using one at a time. By the time I finish this exercise, I feel excellent. Gratitude exercise starts my day with an extremely positive mindset.

CHAPTER 22

Environmental Stimulation

The root of suffering is attachment. Buddha[1]

When environmental stimulation happens, your brain may have doubts after a few days of a smoke-free life. The same people, the same environment, may surround you, not to mention the same stress. Your decisions need to be reliable at this time. When environmental cravings trigger you, it's time you use all the tools that we have discussed in this book. Just remember that once you push the smoking cravings away, your brain becomes stronger. Your ability to say no with confidence is your victory. You may get the trigger to smoke every time you are in a particular environment. However, soon you will realize that triggers are getting weaker and weaker in the same circumstances. The power that controlled you is no more there; the power is with you now. You control what happens to you.

In those split moments of cravings, imagine the results that you are going to achieve. Visualizing them should make you feel terrific, and from this place, you can think clearly. When you push back, associate massive pain with smoking and enormous pleasure with not smoking. We are happy beings by nature, and not smoking should take you back to that nature. Nonsmokers don't feel relief for not smoking. Not smoking is their natural state, and they are content.

Associate pictures of smoking with potential diseases. Associate not smoking with happiness. So every time you even think of smoking, your brain will try to avoid pain and pleasure should soon take over. Keep visualizing the results. All the good times you had in the past with this contrast, and daily practicing of this method, will keep you in a perfect state day after day. You will be able to create this habit of positive thinking and become healthy. If you can make this a part of the morning routine, then it will make your life much easier. This exercise will make all of the processes more relaxed, and you can get the results faster as well. I started with the morning routine, and to this day, I use that time to create new habits and create a healthy, positive mindset for the day.

CHAPTER 23

Morning and Evening Routine

There is nothing impossible to him who will try. Alexander the Great

After a few days of a smoke-free life, you will feel that it is all a mental game. Morning routines and evening routines are the fastest ways to condition the mind. The last thoughts will probably be the first thing you will think when you wake up. I believe that just before going to bed and just after waking up are the two crucial times you can program your mind and set the tone for the day. Evening affirmations can be something like I'm free of nicotine and smoke; I'm about to have an excellent sleep. I'm grateful that I am smoke-free now. I feel healthy. Your morning routine can be doing affirmations while going out for a walk before sunrise. I find this time breathtaking.

You can record some of these affirmations and listen when you go for a run. It can be with any activity in the morning, whether jogging, walking, taking dogs for a walk, or on your commute to work. The morning routine will turbocharge your day and help you to stay focused the whole day. I use this time to do affirmations about health, wealth, prosperity, and to count my blessings. R. A. Emmons and M. E. McCullough (2003)[9] suggest that that a conscious focus on blessings may have emotional and interpersonal benefits. Why don't you create a challenge for yourself to do all these activities for three weeks? It can be done in less than ten minutes or even five minutes if you don't have time.

CHAPTER 24

Having a Positive Mindset

I am the greatest. I said that even before I knew I was. Muhammad Ali[1]

Quitting the habit of smoking is mainly a game of rational thought. Your inability to control your thought patterns can make you not care about the consequences. Not caring about the consequences of being absent from reality makes you repeat what your mind is thinking all the time. I think we know our pattern by now. You may be asking how we can be positive when so many negatives are going around. Well, you can start by being positive about the smallest thing that you can imagine right now. For example, I am alive today; I am happy at this moment; I am breathing; I am healthy. Your momentum of being positive will start immediately. Sometimes it may take longer, depending how fast the negative wheel was rotating. It may have carried lots of energy.

When you start with your positive thoughts exercises, you have stopped the wheel. It may take a bit of time for that wheel to come to a complete stop. You may have seen or heard about major religions where they pray multiple times a day. For instance, religious Muslims pray five times a day, Hindus do so first thing in the morning and evening, and other major religions may have similar rituals that aim to make one present in mind, body, and spirit.

Whether you call source a god, universe, or specific name, it is pointing you to your essence and puts you in the state of a positive mindset. These times allow you to block negative and only connect purely to the source. None of these has to be related to specific religions. It is mainly to copy the structure of practices and employ them into our life. You can actively practice this from moment to moment. When you picture yourself having a good time, the good feeling of being alive will make you feel so close to the source. When you start this exercise last thing at night and first thing in the morning, your desire to be happy will be carried out for the whole morning. This kind of practice could be for a minute or two for five to six times a day. Practice this at least three to five times per day to maintain energy.

CHAPTER 25

How to program your mind

Your past does not equal your future. Tony Robbins[1]

On the second day of not smoking, you may feel a strong desire to forget about everything and start smoking again. These kinds of thoughts are completely normal. This day is significant for you. The action taken today will define what you are going to do next and whether you are going to succeed or not. When the thoughts arise to smoke, it can be hard. Therefore, the idea is to prepare beforehand. Prepare all your affirmations and make them easy to access. Read the affirmations every twenty minutes throughout the day if possible. Bring the thoughts into your attention, like I am healthy now; I am a nonsmoker; I breathe clean air and exhale used nicotine-infused air. Breathing out used air is getting rid of all toxins; nicotine is coming out of my body fast.

Don't worry about statistics on how long it takes to repair. Believe that today all the toxins will be out and you won't suffer anything at all. Do many breathing exercises and drink lots of water. Imagine your body having lots of energy. Today is the day where the impossible is possible. Intention alone will kick-start the repair process. Your body will begin repairing as if it has been restoring your health for weeks and months, and you will feel amazing. Your life will be back on track again. Nothing can distract you. Practice this with every opportunity you get today.

CHAPTER 26

Decision-Making, Giving Up or Giving In

The future belongs to those who prepare for it today. Malcolm X[1]

The idea here is to give up your favorite unhealthy things for a short period or add healthy items. This exercise will help you replace old troublesome habits with healthy ones, and your decision-making ability will improve. If you like coffee, then for five days you may also give up coffee. If you drink soft drinks regularly, then you give them up for five days. This step is not necessary. However, it helped me personally. It's mainly about decision-making and sticking to it. It can be anything, and it does not have to be food or drink related. The same thought pattern will fire when you do this exercise. Once you have success, it will make it easy to apply it as a nonsmoker as well.

What does this have to do with anything, and why are we giving up things that we like? The idea is to deal with the decisions that you have made. You are smoking because your decision-making power has weakened a lot. You quickly give up things now because you are used to not worrying about consequences. You are now able to resist temptations, knowing that it's killing you. You do not think before you react.

The reason you should try this with things you love is so that you can simulate similar experiences regarding smoking. Remember your need for smoking is an illusion, you don't really want to smoke but are compelled to do so due to nicotine addiction. So when you practice with your favorite things, you will be able to trigger the same responses as withdrawal. Every time you get an urge to do your favorite things, fight it and talk yourself out of it. If you can do this consistently for five days, you are ready to change anything. This exercise is provided here to combat bad habits of not following through and strengthens your decision-making abilities, which you may have been neglecting for a long time.

Once you are comfortable with one decision-making process for a few days consistently, you have practiced your decision-making habits. This one change in your life is more powerful than you think, as it can change many habits at once.

CHAPTER 27

Mindfulness Practices and Meditations

The mind, once stretched by a new idea, never returns to its original dimensions. Ralph Waldo Emerson[1]

There are many mindfulness meditations out there. I believe a couple of them will support freeing your mind. If you are more conscious every day, it means you will have a choice of thoughts. When we are unconscious, it's easy to let our thinking drive us into compulsion. It's easy to ignore what's important, and it's effortless to be misguided by your thought patterns. The purpose of the mindfulness exercise includes the following:

- Developing more stable attention and becoming aware of the mind's tendency to go all over the place.
- Creating a small space to observe your thoughts. You can actively choose how to respond instead of merely reacting otherwise.
- Becoming more attuned to your environment—such as with sounds and sights—as it is rather than with mind-made labels.
- To train the attention to stay in the present moment. There are no other moments than the current moment, and this moment is inevitable. In the current moment, the past and future don't exist.

This exercise is compelling and has the potential to change you most profoundly.

Below are some of the mindfulness techniques.

Mindfulness: Waking Up

When you first wake up in the morning, be mindful of your body and feel how each part of your body feels. Take a deep breath and thank the life force for giving you another day. Smile for this beautiful gift of life. Feel your breath for a few moments. Smile and be thankful for all the things that you have, no matter how big or small. You can be grateful for loved ones in your life; grateful for a roof over your head; grateful for your car; thankful for your health; thankful for your eyes, heart, hands, and legs; thankful for an extra day of life; and so forth. Now slowly wake up but feel each part of your body while getting out of bed. Thank your body and your health.

Mindfulness: Showering

When you take a shower, feel the sensation of water touching your skin. Feel the sound and the temperature of the water. What does it feel like? Can you notice the visible and invisible nature? Water not only cleans you, but it also cleanses as well. Appreciate the clean water in your shower. Many people in the world do not even have clean water to drink. However, you are very fortunate. Thank all the people and systems who made it possible for you to enjoy the water and have a shower on demand. Feel every drop of water on your skin. Bring your full attention to the area where water is touching. If you are lost in your thoughts or are starting to plan your day, bring your attention back to the sensations of water.

Mindfulness: Walking

Today plan to do mindful walking in certain areas of you day. For instance, you may have to go to the kitchen to prepare your lunch or breakfast or make your way to a car, train, or bus station. Choose a few areas where you will practice it today. Once you are in that area, pay lots of attention to your walking; feel your feet on the ground. If you start moving automatically, without being aware, bring your attention back to your legs and notice the raising of your legs while walking. Notice the sense of balance. Also try to notice any sounds you are making while walking. Can you hear any sounds around you? What does your body feel at this moment? Is your breathing shallow or heavy? Pay as much attention to your walking as possible. Once you finish this exercise in that particular area, you may carry on with your life.

Mindfulness: Eating

Today, when you are about to eat, set an intention for mindful eating. Before you eat anything, observe the shape, color, how it's sitting on your plate or in your bowl. If possible, take a piece of food and put it in your hand. If the food you are about to eat is not appropriate for this, get a piece of chocolate or any edible item that you can hold. Feel how it feels in your hand. Touch with your other fingers and feel the sensation. Then place the food in your mouth and feel how it feels before you chew. Move it around in your mouth. Notice where the food is in your mouth. Slowly eat and see what sensation you can feel from the food. What are the different flavours? If any thoughts come into your mind, bring your attention back to where you were previously.

Mindfulness: Sounds

Today sit in a comfortable posture and observe any sounds around you. It can be birds chirping; the sound of air conditioning; the sound of falling rain; the humming sound of electronics; or any sound within your body. If you are listening to songs today, please give full attention to them. Observe different instruments playing, observe the voice of the person, and observe the low or high pitch. Observe any pauses between the notes playing. What kind of sound is each instrument making individually? Observe how each sound comes to your attention and then fades away. If any thoughts come into your mind, bring your attention back to where you were previously.

Mindfulness: Seeing

Today observe anything in your sight and notice the shape, color, and size. Have a lot of gratitude just because you can see. Observe anything with lots of appreciation, as not having sight would mean a different world altogether. If you see loved ones, observe them carefully. How do they look? Can you see whether they have any marks on their skin? Do they have curly hair? What hair color do they have? Can you observe the shapes of their noses? How do they look when they smile? Do this exercise discreetly, of course, in case you make them uncomfortable. Anything you see today, observe with lots of curiosity. Look at everything today without any labels.

Observe the trees with leaves and branches. Observe each leaf, how it's thriving with life, and watch how all the leaves are hanging in the branches. If you get to see water today, pay close attention to it. Observe the size of the ripples, if there are any. Observe its calmness. Can you feel the water? Can you see the invisible nature and visible nature? What else can you notice about the water? Observe what's there, without any labels. Look at the evening sky and morning sky. Watch the clouds and the stars at night. Keep observing today with absolute attention. If any thoughts come into your mind, bring attention back to where you were before.

Mindfulness: Body Observation

Lie down on the ground for a couple of minutes today. Close your eyes. Put your attention in every part of your body one place at a time. Begin with your feet. Stretch your feet for five seconds. Put your consciousness in your feet and feel the feelings. Stay for a couple of moments. Now shift your consciousness to your ankles. See if you can feel a tingling sensation for a time. If you can't feel that, that's all right. Now transfer your consciousness to the calves. Squeeze the muscles of your calves; feel the sensations for five seconds. Now for five seconds, move your awareness to the knees. For five seconds, squeeze your thigh muscles and feel the feelings. Now move your consciousness to the genital area. Press the muscles of the stomach and shift your consciousness. Squeeze your chest now and place your consciousness there. Do the same for your back and shoulders. Clamp your hands for five seconds. Feel the awareness shifting to the fingertips from your shoulder on each side. Now, by squeezing the muscles, move your attention to the neck muscles. Squeeze the muscles of your face by making silly faces and shift your consciousness there.

Transfer your awareness to the top of your head. Wait a few moments. Breathe deeply and relax. In reverse order, push your awareness to your feet from the top of your head. Notice all of your body's sensations. Repeat the process but this time quickly move your awareness from your feet all the way to your head and back to your feet, seeing if you can observe all the sensations as energy moves all around your body.

Mindfulness: Breathing

Today plan to take two minutes of every hour or every two hours and be mindful of your breath. Feel the inhalation of air in and out. Observe what it feels like in your nose, chest area, and in your stomach area. Does your stomach rise when you inhale? Does it fall back when you exhale? Between inhalation and exhalation, are there any pauses in between?

When you inhale, take a deeper breath than usual; the same with exhalation. Observe the breath for two minutes and then carry on with your day-to-day activities. This mindfulness technique is discreet, and no one may even notice that you are observing your breath. If any thoughts come into your mind, bringing attention back to your breath.

Mindfulness: Going to Bed

When you are ready to go to bed, mindfully walk towards your bed. Once you lie down, feel the bed with parts of your body. Feel all the sensations of the bed and your bedding. Feel the warm sensations. If any thoughts come into your mind, bring attention back to where you were. Find a few things in your day that made you happy. It could be as simple as talking with your children, having a coffee, eating lunch, talking with someone. Go back to that moment in your mind. Enjoy the sensations of warmth and good feeling. Soak in this moment and be thankful.

Mindfulness: Love

Today use your loved ones as a way of meditation, whether it's your partner, your kids, or your pets. Close your eyes and observe the love you have for that person, pet, or what have you. What does this love feel like? Where did this love come from? Did you already have it? In the case of a person, with the likely exception of a baby in the womb, you didn't have this love for them before you met. Just be in this space and observe. This love was already there within you. The only difference is that you expressed it to someone else. As you were capable of loving, you met your loved ones.

The love you have for your children or pets was already there within you. If you didn't have that love, you wouldn't be able to love them. If you are capable of this love, then you are capable of a lot more regarding everything around you. Try to feel that love and see if you can include everything and everyone within it. If you detested someone, see if you can shine towards them the love you have. The hatred and envy that you would otherwise have felt before will melt in front of your eyes. The choice to love yourself and others is within you. You already have love; you just need to expand it to include everyone.

Start with the love for this person, pet, or whatever it is, and use the same love to include all your family and friends. Expand that love to neighbors. Feel the love first and add them to it one by one. Now expand that love to everyone and everything in your area. You can apply and extend your love to anything around you, like trees, lakes, plants, grass, cats, dogs, birds, and so forth. Include everyone and everything in your suburb, state, and other countries in your love. Expand that love to the whole world and then expand that to the moon, sun, stars, and the entire universe.

Stay in this love for a few minutes and soak in the moment. Notice that love you have for you and others is endless and can include the whole universe. You have infinite potential to love everyone. You are in control of how much love you want to give to others. Love is there, and you will want to include everyone in it. Now you can slowly open your eyes.

This meditation is compelling, and it will melt hatred, envy, and emotional trauma away from you and make you realize the power you have to love everyone.

CHAPTER 28

The Thirty-Day Challenge

Do something worth remembering. Elvis Presley[1]

These are the steps to follow every day for thirty days.

Morning:

- Begin your morning with a thirty minute routine, preferably a one hour routine.
- Do affirmations related to quitting smoke as highlighted in the chapter "Morning and Evening Routine" for five minutes. Use all your five senses to feel the emotions and feelings while doing it. Increase your affirmation time to ten minutes if your routine is for one hour.
- Feel your good image for a few minutes and meditate on this for five minutes. Feel yourself being more attuned to your good image. Increase the feel good image exercise time to ten minutes if your routine is for one hour.

- Exercise doing push-ups, squats, running, yoga, or any physical activities for five minutes. Increase the exercise time to ten minutes if your routine is for one hour. If you don't want to increase for another ten minutes, you can read a book or listen to audiobooks for another ten minutes.
- Practice diminishing anchors for five minutes in all your identified places. Increase the diminishing anchor exercise time to ten minutes if your routine is for one hour.
- Do any mindfulness meditation for five minutes. Increase your mindfulness time to ten minutes if your routine is for one hour.
- Use the remaining five minutes for breathing and being present exercise. Increase your breathing and being present exercise time to ten minutes if your routine is for one hour.

Throughout the day:

- Remind yourself how healthy you are since you quit, every twenty minutes if possible.
- Remind yourself how healing has started and is repairing every cell.
- Practice reminding yourself of your good image at least sixty times in your mind today.
- Practice being present in ten things you do today. It can be while eating, walking, talking, working, talking on the phone, and so forth.
- Give up one of your bad habits or add one healthy habit for a month. As mentioned earlier, it can be giving up soft drinks for a whole month or giving up coffee if that is the trigger. If you are having coffee, perhaps give up sugar in your coffee and replace it with something else. Every individual is different; however, cutting one habit and sticking with it for a month will strengthen your decision-making abilities, which will help in many areas of your life. If you are not giving anything up, perhaps you can add one litre of water to your daily intake, provided you don't exceed amounts recommended by your health care professional, or add any other good habit. It can be anything. Look into your life and see what is bothering you or what will make your experience better and make the change accordingly for a month.

Evening:

- Practice affirmations for five minutes.
- Do any mindfulness meditation for five minutes.
- Soak in the moment of being grateful and conquering the day without smoking. Feel the cells repairing and nicotine cravings disappearing from your body for good.

The above steps are only suggestions, and you can personalize as needed. This thirty-day challenge will help you in many areas of your life. Not only will you conquer quitting smoking, but you will also repair your lungs, your mind, and your attitude all at once, in addition to your overall health and the ability to love yourself.

After thirty days, you may be a completely different person. This challenge has improved my health and mind from a terrible state to an awesome state. It helped me in many different areas of my life and improved my relationships with my wife, children, and friends immensely. My friends, colleagues, and family all saw drastic changes in my life, almost beyond recognition. These changes were happening in many areas of my life simultaneously.

Conclusion

You are what you believe yourself to be. Paulo Coelho[1]

Lots of information out there can make it seem as if after reading a book, you can automatically quit. In reality, you need to understand your mind and thoughts. You need a systematic approach to apply and deal with the problem in a specific manner so that you can eliminate negative associations and add positive ones. This book provides practical exercises that you can apply and is not only limited to quitting smoking. You can use the techniques mentioned here in many parts of your life. We will need to address any emotional abuse or the number of positive relaxation thoughts associated with your addiction. In reality, these are all illusions. Either way, it's killing you. If you have linked addiction to emotional abuse, you are killing yourself twice as fast—one from the emotional issue and one from smoking a cigarette. The outcome is not good either way, so let's remove the issues itself, starting from its roots.

Many people say that they have tried everything, like nicotine patches, nicotine gum, and nicotine spray, and have tried to quit numerous times. There may be information out there claiming that you don't need to do anything other than reading or listening. I think those are only one part of the story. Spending some time finding out about how your patterns trigger you and how to associate a good image and remove bad ones will take you much further than you think. How you get to the finish line is different from completing the task. Just remember, the desire was created a long time back to quit smoking, as you were becoming aware of the health implications. Until you reach the flipping point, you might still ignore the health risks. All the past times that you have tried to give up smoking and probably failed has led you to this access point, and there's no looking back now. You tried quitting smoking, and you decided to get stronger. You changed the way you looked at smoking. You learned more about yourself. If you desire to quit smoking, you can. If you wish to keep smoking, you can. The mind is so powerful that you can accomplish anything you want.

It's time to trust your instincts and figure it out by yourself by knowing your patterns rather than adding pills straightaway. If it's needed, then it's Okey; however, please explore your habits so you can make a longer-lasting change. Our minds are a lot more powerful than we believe. It's time to replace compulsion in our lives with choice.

Welcome to your brand-new life.

References

1. Maxime Lagacé. (November 13, 2019). *420 BEST FAMOUS QUOTES BY FAMOUS PEOPLE (ALIVE AND DEAD)*. Available: https://wisdomquotes.com/famous-quotes/. Last accessed 18th Nov 2019

2. U.S. Department of Health and Human Services. "The Health Consequences of Smoking—50 Years of Progress: A Report of the Surgeon General." 2014. Atlanta: U.S. Department of Health and Human Services, Centers for Disease Control and Prevention, National Center for Chronic Disease Prevention and Health Promotion, Office on Smoking and Health [accessed April 20 2017].

3. U.S. Department of Health and Human Services. "How Tobacco Smoke Causes Disease: What It Means to You." 2010. Atlanta: U.S. Department of Health and Human Services, Centers for Disease Control and Prevention, National Center for Chronic Disease Prevention and Health Promotion, Office on Smoking and Health [accessed April 20, 2017].

4. Centers for Disease Control and Prevention. QuickStats. "Number of Deaths from 10 Leading Causes—National Vital Statistics System," United States. 2010. Morbidity and Mortality Weekly Report 2013:62(08); 155 [accessed April 2017].

5. Mokdad, A. H., J. S. Marks, D. F. Stroup, and J. L. Gerberding. "Actual Causes of Death in the United States." *JAMA: Journal of the American Medical Association*, 2004: 291(10):1238–45 [cited April 20, 2017].

6. U.S. Department of Health and Human Services. "Women and Smoking: A Report of the Surgeon General." 2001. Rockville, Maryland: U.S. Department of Health and Human Services, Public Health Service, Office of the Surgeon General. 2001 [accessed April 20, 2017].

7. U.S. Department of Health and Human Services. "Reducing the Health Consequences of Smoking: 25 Years of Progress: A Report of the Surgeon General." 1989. Rockville, Maryland: U.S. Department of Health and Human Services, Public Health Service, Centers for Disease Control, National Center for Chronic Disease Prevention and Health Promotion, Office on Smoking and Health, 1989 [accessed 2017 Apr 20].

8. Lyubomirsky, S. 2010. The How of happiness: A New Approach to Getting the Life You Want. Sydney: Hachette.

9. Emmons, R. A., and M. E. McCullough. 2003. "Counting Blessings Versus Burdens: An Experimental Investigation of Gratitude and Subjective Well-Being in Daily Life." *Journal of Personality and Social Psychology*, 84(2), 377–89.

10. Bratman, Gregory N., J. Paul Hamilton et al. 2015. "Nature Experience Reduces Rumination and Subgenual Prefrontal Cortex Activation." Available at https://www.pnas.org/content/112/28/8567 [last accessed August 24, 2019].

11. Anthony Robbins. (2003). Mastering Your Mind: How to Run Your Brain. In: Applebome, P and Golden, H *Unlimited Power*. New York: Simon & Schuster, Inc. 102.